The Library of Sexual Health™

URINARY TRACT INFECTIONS

KRISTA WEST

The Rosen Publishing Group, Inc., New York

Published in 2007 by The Rosen Publishing Group, Inc.
29 East 21st Street, New York, NY 10010

First Edition

Library of Congress Cataloging-in-Publication Data

West, Krista.
Urinary tract infections/Krista West.
   p. cm.—(The library of sexual health)
Includes bibliographical references and index.
ISBN-13: 978-1-4042-0905-3
ISBN-10: 1-4042-0905-0 (library binding)
1. Urinary tract infections—Juvenile literature. I. Title. II. Series.
RC901.8.W47 2006
616.6—dc22

               2006002096

Manufactured in the United States of America

CONTENTS

Introduction 4

Chapter One What Is a UTI? 7

Chapter Two Who Gets UTIs? 17

Chapter Three Determining If You Have a UTI 28

Chapter Four Getting Help for a UTI 35

Chapter Five Living with a UTI 44

Glossary 54

For More Information 56

For Further Reading 60

Bibliography 61

Index 63

INTRODUCTION

U rinary tract infections, or UTIs, are a type of infection that has likely plagued humans for thousands of years. UTIs are extremely uncomfortable, very common, and particularly widespread, affecting millions of people every year. The urinary tract system makes, stores, and expels urine, one of the waste products of the human body. Every human has one. And every human uses the system daily.

Infections occur when bacteria enter the urinary tract system and trigger lots of problems. The UTI can be what doctors call uncomplicated, a mere inconvenience causing frequent and painful urination. Or it can be a complicated infection, leading to life-threatening kidney problems if it is left untreated.

Treatment most often entails a series of antibiotics to kill off the infectious bacteria. In most cases, the correct series of antibiotics can treat the physical ailment effectively. On the emotional side, there are steps you can take to manage the feelings of frustration or embarrassment that you might experience if you have a UTI, or lots of

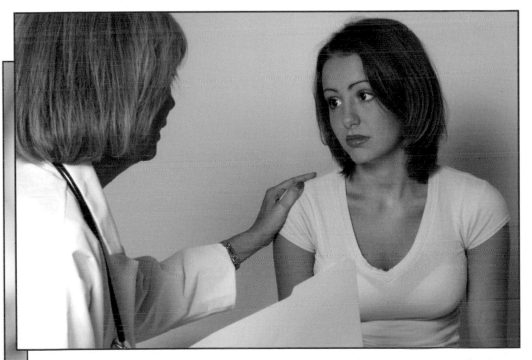

A doctor explains what to expect to a young woman with a urinary tract infection. Frequent and painful urination are not uncommon in cases of uncomplicated UTIs such as this one.

UTIs. If you've never heard of UTIs, you aren't alone. And if you have a UTI, you aren't alone, either.

Experts suggest that UTIs are one of the most common reasons people make a trip to the doctor. In the United States alone, the American Urological Association says at least eight million people see the doctor for UTI treatment each year. Of this number, about three-quarters are women. (Statistics for teen girls with UTIs as a group are currently unavailable.) As indicated by Andrew L. Freedman in *Urologic Diseases in America*, 24 out of 100,000 adolescents, ages eleven to seventeen, were hospitalized for UTIs in the United States in 2000.

But despite the number of people dealing with these infections (about 150 million people worldwide every year, according to Paul Iannini, clinical professor of medicine at Yale University School of Medicine, in his book *Contemporary Diagnosis and Management of Urinary Tract Infections*), most people don't know much about them. This introduction to the urinary tract system will help explain how and when your system can be infected, and guide you to find and understand various treatments for UTIs.

CHAPTER ONE

What Is a UTI?

A urinary tract infection occurs when bacteria grow in your urinary tract. These invasive bacteria can come from your own skin, from sexual activity, and from using certain forms of birth control. The trick to avoiding a UTI is to keep these bacteria at bay. Urine is normally sterile—it is free of bacteria of any kind. In most cases when bacteria get into places they aren't supposed to be, the body's immune system removes them without a problem. But sometimes the immune system cannot fight bacteria in the urinary tract, allowing infections to grow in the system and cause problems. Your gender, age, health, and behavior all play a role in whether or not you get a UTI at some point in your lifetime. Understanding what a UTI is and how you get one can help you avoid it—and know how to deal with it if you do get one.

THE URINARY TRACT SYSTEM

The urinary tract system includes four connected parts: the kidneys, ureters, bladder, and urethra. Men and

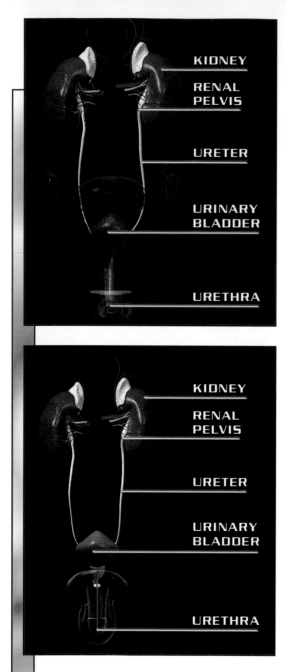

KIDNEY

RENAL PELVIS

URETER

URINARY BLADDER

URETHRA

KIDNEY

RENAL PELVIS

URETER

URINARY BLADDER

URETHRA

The kidneys filter wastes from the blood and create urine. The ureters carry the urine to the bladder where it is stored until you urinate. Urine passes through the urethra when it leaves the body. The internal system is the same in women and men.

women have the same four parts in the body. Together, the parts of the urinary tract system create and store urine until you urinate. Each part has a specific job.

Most people have two kidneys that are each about the size of a closed fist and filter waste materials from your blood; these wastes become urine. The ureters are tubes that carry urine from the kidneys to the bladder, a flexible, muscular sack. The balloon-like bladder stores urine until you urinate. The urethra is the tube that connects the bladder to the outside of your body. When you urinate, the bladder muscles contract to squeeze urine through the urethra and out of the body. The kidneys and ureters are known as the upper urinary tract. The bladder and urethra are known as the lower urinary tract.

Bacteria

Bacteria are ultra-tiny, one-celled organisms that can be seen only with a powerful microscope. There are many different types of bacteria. Some bacteria in your body are useful (including the ones that break down food during digestion). Others are harmful (including the ones that cause food poisoning and diarrhea).

The most common causes of UTIs are the bacteria that live in the digestive system (the stomach and intestines), on the skin around the rectum (where solid wastes exit the body), and in the reproductive system of women, including the vagina (the birth canal).

Bacteria in the digestive system can migrate into the urinary tract and cause infection. This type of UTI is not caught like a cold from other people; it happens when naturally helpful bacteria get into the wrong place.

Bacteria in the reproductive system can also travel into the urinary tract and cause infection. Both reproductive and digestive system bacteria can be passed between partners during sexual intercourse and cause UTIs. Sexually active women are more likely to become infected than sexually active men. Researchers do not totally understand why women are more susceptible to UTIs than men, but they believe that it might be because of anatomy—that bacteria have a shorter distance to travel

Myths and Facts

When it comes to UTIs, it's sometimes hard to distinguish fact from fiction. Here are some debunked myths to set the record straight:

MYTH: UTIs can be uncomfortable, but they're not serious.
FACT: UTIs can kill you if they are left untreated. Over time, the infection can get into your kidneys and other parts of your body, causing permanent damage.

MYTH: Every person who gets a UTI will have the same set of symptoms.
FACT: Not everyone with a UTI experiences the same symptoms, but most people get a few symptoms (such as pain during urination). However, it is possible to have a UTI with no symptoms at all.

MYTH: Keeping the genital area clean will prevent a UTI.
FACT: Although some experts say showering and urinating after sex (to wash away unwanted bacteria) can help prevent a UTI, there is no scientific research to back it up.

MYTH: Only grown-ups get UTIs.
FACT: Anyone, anywhere, can get a UTI, including babies, teens, adults, and the elderly.

MYTH: You can't get a UTI from having sex.
FACT: Some UTIs can be sexually transmitted; it depends on what type of bacteria fuel your UTI.

MYTH: Men and boys don't get UTIs.
FACT: Anyone, anywhere, can get a UTI, including boys and men.

from the rectum to the urinary tract system in women. The UTI-causing bacteria can be introduced during sex from the vagina, spermicides, creams, diaphragms, or other objects.

The bacteria found in the digestive system are different from those found in the reproductive system. There are four main types of bacteria that cause UTIs, but *Escherichia coli* (*E. coli*) is the most common cause. Viruses, fungi, and parasites can also cause UTIs, but these cases are less common.

Digestive System Bacteria

E. coli comes in hundreds of different forms. One form lives naturally in our digestive system and helps break down the food we eat. Other forms are present in uncooked meat and cause severe illness or even death when eaten by humans. These forms of *E. coli* can get into the urinary tract and cause an infection.

The naturally beneficial *E. coli* in the digestive system can exit the body in our solid waste. When bacteria from these solid wastes get onto the skin, they can migrate into the urinary tract system through the urethra and create an infection.

When humans eat meat containing potentially lethal forms of *E. coli*, these bacteria also end up in the solid wastes produced by the digestive system and travel to the urinary tract in the same way. Research into how this form of *E. coli* creates UTIs is ongoing.

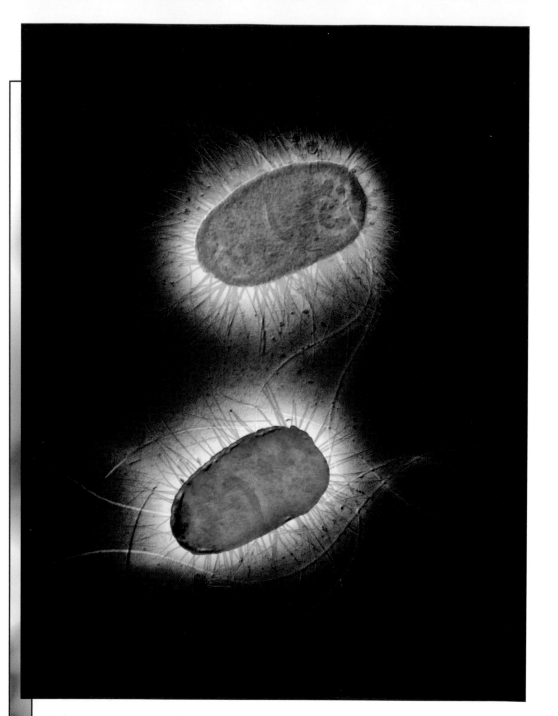

These microscopic *Escherichia coli* (*E. coli*) bacteria are the most common bacteria that cause UTIs. They are naturally present in the digestive system but cause infection in the urinary tract. Hundreds of thousands of bacteria can fit into the period at the end of this sentence.

Staphylococcus saprophyticus (*S. saprophyticus*) is a bacterium found in animals and animal carcasses, but it is rarely found in healthy humans. Scientists are still studying how it gets into humans, but it probably enters the digestive tract as food, travels to the skin through solid wastes, and migrates into the urinary tract.

These two types of bacteria cause most UTIs. *E. coli* causes about 80 percent and *S. saprophyticus* is responsible for 5 to 15 percent of all UTIs in adults in the United States, according to the American Urological Association. Infections caused by these bacteria are not contagious— they cannot be caught from a stranger passing by on the street or through casual physical contact.

Reproductive System Bacteria

Chlamydia trachomatis (*C. trachomatis*) is one of the smallest types of bacteria on Earth and lives inside human cells. These bacteria are not normally present in the reproductive system but can cause the sexually transmitted disease (STD) chlamydia and an eye disease called trachoma, which can cause blindness if it is not treated. The bacteria can also migrate to the urinary tract system to create a UTI. Women whose reproductive systems are infected with chlamydia (the STD) may have no symptoms at all, or they may experience increased vaginal discharge. Many men who are infected may not experience any symptoms at all, or they may experience a burning feeling while urinating. Those with urinary tract systems infected with chlamydia (the same bacteria but in a different place) will have a UTI.

Mycoplasma hominis (M. hominis) is a bacterium that lives in the vagina. During sex these bacteria can be transferred to skin, where they can then migrate to the urinary tract system and cause infection. UTIs caused by C. trachomatis and M. hominis are less common than digestive system bacterial causes, but exact statistics for these bacteria are unknown. Both C. trachomatis and M. hominis can be transferred between partners during sexual intercourse.

There are many other types of bacteria that can cause UTIs, including Neisseria gonorrhoeae (the bacteria that cause the STD known as gonorrhea), but none live normally in the urinary tract system. All cause infections when introduced to the wrong place.

SEVERITY OF INFECTION

The severity of a UTI depends on where in the urinary tract system the infection occurs. Lower urinary tract infections are considered uncomplicated or simple, while upper urinary tract infections are more complicated.

Uncomplicated UTIs

Uncomplicated UTIs occur in the lower urinary tract, which includes the urethra and bladder. The lower urinary tract is where bacteria enter the body, and infections are usually treated before moving further up in the urinary tract system. There are two main types of uncomplicated UTIs.

Urethritis is an infection limited to the urethra. It can be caused by bacteria or by a chemical irritant (such as a contraceptive cream). Urethritis can cause painful and frequent urination.

Cystitis is a chronic infection in the bladder. According to the American Urological Association, most cystitis cases in the United States (about 80 percent) are caused by the *E. coli* bacteria. This infection can cause painful and frequent urination, plus cloudy, bloody, or strong-smelling urine. Pelvic pain, pain during sex, and fevers can also result. Most people who get uncomplicated UTIs do not experience cystitis.

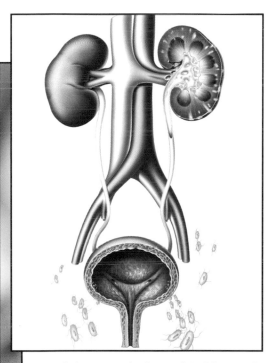

E. coli bacteria (indicated in blue, and not to scale) attack the bladder wall causing a condition known as cystitis. If not treated, the bacteria will move up the ureters to the kidneys, potentially causing permanent kidney damage.

Complicated UTIs

Complicated UTIs occur in the upper urinary tract, which includes the ureters and kidneys. If an uncomplicated UTI is left untreated, bacteria from the lower urinary tract can migrate to the upper urinary tract. There is one main type of complicated UTI known as pyelonephritis.

Pyelonephritis is an infection of the kidneys. Pyelonephritis usually starts in the urethra or bladder and travels to the kidneys. This infection can develop suddenly, known as an acute condition. Or it can be chronic, lasting a long time without clearing up. Severe stomach pain, back pain, fevers, and fatigue can occur.

Pyelonephritis is the most severe type of UTI and can permanently damage kidneys or even be fatal. There are few reliable statistics on how many people get pyelonephritis each year, but the National Kidney Foundation of East Tennessee in Knoxville reports that 60,000 people die each year in the United States from kidney and urinary illnesses.

CHAPTER TWO

Who Gets UTIs?

Anyone can get a UTI at any stage of life, but there are big differences between men and women as far as when they can develop UTIs. Boys get UTIs more than girls during the first three months of life, but after this period healthy boys and men are far less likely to get UTIs. Girls can develop UTIs beginning at age two and older, and women get UTIs more often than men. According to the Pennsylvania State University Hershey Medical Center, one in five women will develop a UTI at least once during her life, and many of them will have more than one.

Doctors suspect that the basic anatomy of women makes them naturally more prone to UTIs. In women, the physical opening of the urinary tract system is very close to the openings of the digestive and reproductive systems, two places where bacteria enter and exit the body. When bacteria from these two systems get on the skin, they don't have far to migrate into the urinary tract in women. Other than gender, the three main factors that affect your chances of developing a urinary tract infection are age, health, and behavior.

Age

UTIs occur most often during three stages of life: the first years of life, the last years of life, and times of sexual activity in women.

According to the National Kidney and Urologic Diseases Information Clearinghouse in Bethesda, Maryland, 1.78 million people, age twenty or older, were hospitalized in the United States in 2001 with urinary tract infections, and of that number, 1.29 million were women. When women reach an age that they become sexually active, they get more UTIs. It doesn't matter if the age is thirteen or forty-three—all sexually active women are more vulnerable to UTIs. During sexual intercourse, bacteria from the vagina and rectum can enter the urinary tract system through the urethra. Certain forms of birth control are known to increase the chances of developing a UTI as well (for more information about methods of birth control and UTIs, see the following section on behavior).

Babies can get UTIs due to anatomic abnormalities. Uncircumcised boys are commonly affected because they have high bacterial counts in the area near the foreskin. As the body develops and abnormalities are corrected, the number of UTIs in boys and girls decreases.

Elderly people often get UTIs because of a decrease in the ability of the urinary tract to function efficiently. When

Men and women of all ages can get a UTI, but sexually active women are more vulnerable. Experts estimate that about one-third of all women in the United States are diagnosed with a UTI before they reach the age of twenty-four.

this happens, a flexible tube called a catheter is sometimes inserted to extract urine from the bladder. Catheters are known to be a major cause of UTIs, but not just in the elderly. Catheters are often used on patients—including teens—after surgery. Most medical experts, including those at the University of Maryland Medical Center, say that catheter-induced UTIs are very common, catheters should be used only when it is positively necessary, and

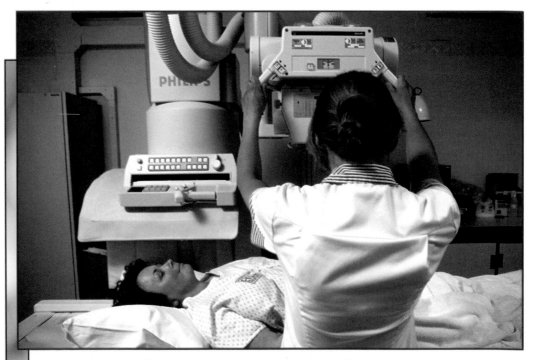

A nurse takes an X-ray of a woman's urinary tract, called a urogram or a pyelogram. In most cases of uncomplicated UTIs, a urogram is not usually necessary, but it is very useful in evaluating women who have recurring UTIs. The procedure involves injecting a vein in a patient's arm with a contrast dye and then taking several X-rays to watch the dye as it moves through the kidneys, ureters, and bladder.

they should be removed as quickly as possible. If you are headed to the hospital for surgery, ask your doctor about ways to prevent a catheter-induced UTI.

HEALTH

Any health condition that changes the operation of the body's normal systems gives people a higher chance of developing a UTI—specifically, any condition that affects the immune system or the urinary tract. Diabetes (because it affects the immune system) and pregnancy (because it affects the urinary tract) both get special attention when it comes to UTIs.

Diabetes can do three things to the body that make it more susceptible to UTIs. First, diabetes affects the body's immune system by slowing down the circulation of the blood. This slowed circulation reduces the ability of infection-fighting blood cells to get where they need to go in the body. Second, people with diabetes often have bladders that don't work very well, allowing urine to collect bacteria and foster their growth. And third, according to the National Kidney Foundation, headquartered in New York City, the urine of people with diabetes has a high sugar content. This encourages the growth of bacteria and kidney infection.

Being pregnant is no more likely to cause an uncomplicated UTI than not being pregnant. However, as reported by the National Kidney and Urologic Disease Information Clearinghouse, when a pregnant woman does get a UTI, it is more likely to travel to her kidneys. For this reason, some doctors test the urine repeatedly during pregnancy. Diabetes and pregnancy are the two most widely recognized health conditions affecting your chance of getting a UTI, but any disease that has an impact on the immune system (including AIDS) is a concern.

BEHAVIOR

The two leading behavioral causes of UTIs are sexual activity (particularly in young women) and the use of catheters in hospital patients.

Amee Manges, assistant professor of epidemiology, biostatistics, and occupational health at McGill University in Montreal, Quebec, said in an interview on December 16, 2005, that sexual intercourse is the strongest risk factor for developing a UTI in young women. Manges is an expert in reproductive infections in women, and devotes much of her time to studying UTIs. Manges says sex increases the occurrence of UTIs by moving bacteria (such as *E. coli*) from the skin or vagina to the urinary tract, or when certain birth control methods are used.

During sexual intercourse, bacteria can be transferred from the vagina to the skin, where they can migrate into the urinary tract. These bacteria are already present in the body; having sex just helps move them around. In this case, the movement of bacteria is somewhat unavoidable.

Certain methods of birth control can cause UTIs in a very different way. Foreign bacteria can be introduced to

Ten Facts About UTIs

1. The average adult passes about a quart and a half of urine per day.

2. About eight million people in the United States develop a UTI each year.

3. One in five women will develop a UTI at some point in her lifetime.

4. About 5 percent of girls in the United States will get a UTI sometime before they graduate from high school.

5. Young women who get a UTI have a 30 to 50 percent chance of getting another one.

6. The overall lifetime risk of getting a UTI is high (greater than 50 percent for all adult women). The risk percentage for men is unavailable; however, about 20 percent of all UTIs occur in men, according to *Urologic Diseases in America* (2004).

7. Sexual activity is the number-one risk factor for young women to develop UTIs.

8. Boys can get UTIs in the first three months of life. After that, UTIs are rare in young men.

9. In the United States, *Escherichia coli* (*E. coli*) causes about 80 percent of UTIs in adults and more than 80 percent of acute UTIs in children ages seventeen and younger.

10. Oral antibiotic treatment cures 85 percent of uncomplicated UTIs.

the system by diaphragms, spermicides, or other objects. In these instances, the introduction of bacteria can sometimes be avoided.

According to many research studies, women who use diaphragms (the molded rubber cap-like devices that are fitted over the cervix before sexual intercourse) are more likely to get UTIs than women who use other forms of birth control. The diaphragm, which is used with a contraceptive jelly, can press on the neck of the bladder, preventing it from emptying completely and leaving a pool of unmoving urine in which bacteria can grow. Inserting and removing the diaphragm can also introduce bacteria to the urinary tract.

Recently, studies have found that women whose partners use condoms with spermicidal foam also tend to have high growth rates of bacteria in the vagina. Such foams kill off the beneficial bacteria naturally present in a woman's system, making room for infection-causing bacteria to grow. Condoms and spermicides are effective at preventing other types of STDs and pregnancy, but people should be aware that some spermicidal use has been associated with an increased risk of getting a UTI in sexually active women.

While sexual activity is the leading risk factor for young women in getting UTIs, the use of catheters in hospital patients is another major cause. If you're using a catheter for a medical reason in a hospital, you might be more prone to getting a UTI.

PREVENTING A UTI

Some people are more prone to get UTIs than others for unknown reasons. However, doctors agree that some simple steps can be taken to help fend off infection. Each of the recommended steps helps expel urine from the body (eliminating a place for bacteria to grow) or keeps bacteria away from the urinary tract (removing the opportunity for an infection to begin).

The National Kidney and Urologic Disease Information Clearinghouse (NKUDIC) in the United States and the Kidney Foundation of Canada (KFC) advise taking these preventative steps for reducing the chance of getting UTIs:

- Drink plenty of water every day (at least six glasses) so that you urinate often.
- Empty your bladder completely when needed so bacteria have little chance of growing.
- Urinate after sexual intercourse to flush bacteria out of the system (this step is especially important for women).
- Wipe yourself from front to back so as not to transport bacteria from solid wastes to your urethra. (Although the NKUDC and KFC both recommend this step, some experts say it has not been medically proven to prevent UTIs.)
- Avoid baths and take showers instead (in a bath, you are sitting in water that becomes filled with bacteria). (Both the NKUDC and KFC suggest this tip as a pre- ventative measure, but it has not been scientifically proven to help.)

In addition to these widely accepted preemptive methods, some doctors suggest drinking cranberry juice, which is thought to be effective in fighting bacteria. It was once believed that cranberry juice made urine more acidic, killing harmful bacteria. New studies suggest the remedy is slightly more complicated.

Healthy Living

Cranberries and urinary infections

A new study confirms the widespread belief that cranberry juice can help beat urinary tract infections.

Who's at risk?

■ Women between 25 and 29 and those over 55 are most likely to have a urinary tract infection

■ Up to 60% of women have had a urinary infection at some time; one-third had a recurrence within the next year

Why cranberries work

■ Research suggests that a chemical in cranberries related to tannin may keep E. coli and other bacteria from attaching to human cells and causing infection

© 2001 KRT

Source: British Medical Journal
Graphic: Ulla Knudsen, Lee Hulteng

Some scientific evidence shows that drinking cranberry juice can help prevent UTIs by stopping bacteria from adhering to the walls of the urinary tract, although the remedy is not yet medically proven.

A project sponsored by the National Institutes of Health, a medical research agency within the U.S. Department of Health and Human Services, is investigating the ability of cranberries to prevent the adhesion of bacteria to the walls of the urinary tract. If bacteria can't adhere to the system, they cannot grow and cause infection.

CHAPTER THREE

Determining If You Have a UTI

UTI symptoms can be different for everyone. It isn't always easy to talk about how you are feeling, but you are not alone if you have a UTI.

W hen you have a sore throat, the skin lining your throat becomes red and irritated, causing discomfort. Most of us are familiar with this pain and what it feels like. And we usually know what it means.

When you have a UTI, the same red, irritating soreness happens in parts of your urinary tract. In this case, most of us are unfamiliar with this pain and what it feels like. And we don't know what it means.

Exactly how a UTI feels depends on the severity of the infection and on the response from each individual's body. Some people can be infected without even realizing it. Others are forced to stay home from school or work because the pain is so severe.

Angela Kilmartin, a writer and advocate of UTI education, was unable to recognize the symptoms when she got her first UTI; like most people, she was unaware of the potential severity of the infection. She soon learned how severe and disruptive the pain of recurrent UTIs can be.

Kilmartin's doctor diagnosed her UTI and she began antibiotic treatment to kill the infecting bacteria. For five years she battled a new UTI every two to three weeks. During this time, Kilmartin realized she was particularly susceptible to UTIs. She contended with not only the UTIs, but also the uncomfortable side effects accompanying the drugs.

After a while, Kilmartin learned to recognize her symptoms and developed her own methods to prevent the infections before they began. She wrote seven books about UTIs and related problems, began a support group, and started a support group newsletter devoted to UTI sufferers. According to Kilmartin, the first step in fighting a UTI is learning to recognize the symptoms. Look for these symptoms to determine whether or not you have a UTI.

text continues on page 31

Jackie's Story

One day several months ago, seventeen-year-old Jackie Mendez started getting a burning sensation whenever she urinated. And she seemed to go to the bathroom more often than usual. Jackie didn't think much of the new inconvenience. It was no big deal.

After about five days, Jackie became nauseous and developed a low fever. She missed a day of school for the first time since the seventh grade. She took some over-the-counter painkillers for the fever, ate some crackers to soothe her stomach, and made it to school the rest of the week. But something wasn't right.

Jackie felt a little embarrassed. No one at home or school talked about having problems urinating. But she needed information. Jackie decided to see the school nurse. Maybe she could answer some questions.

"It burns when I go to the bathroom," Jackie explained as she tried to describe the pain, "and I feel sick all the time." The nurse immediately asked for more details: how often did Jackie go to the bathroom; when did the pain begin; was Jackie sexually active? Jackie was shocked by the last question—that's not what she came to talk about.

"You might have a urinary tract infection," the nurse explained, "they are really common among girls your age." Common? Jackie thought to herself. She'd never heard of a UTI before. "A lot of girls at this school have the same symptoms as you," the nurse continued. "It can be caused by bacteria in the food you eat or by sexual activity. And some people just get UTIs more than others; no one really knows why." A lot of girls here have UTIs? Jackie never heard anyone talk about it. The nurse suggested Jackie make an appointment with her doctor.

Jackie thought about what the nurse said and decided to talk to her father about seeing the doctor. Her mother was out of town on a business trip for another week and Jackie didn't want to wait that long. Perhaps her infection wasn't something to be embarrassed about after all. They scheduled a doctor's appointment.

The doctor asked the same questions the nurse had asked her at school, so Jackie felt prepared to answer. "Sounds like we need a urine sample," the doctor said as he pulled a small, sealed plastic cup from a drawer. "Just follow the directions in the bathroom and give this to the nurse. We'll call you tomorrow."

The doctor explained that they would test the urine for bacteria, a clear sign of a UTI. If he needed to see Jackie for a pelvic examination, the office would call to make another appointment. On the way home, Jackie and her father stopped to pick up a prescription of antibiotics. The doctor suggested taking them just in case.

By the next morning Jackie already felt better than she had in weeks. The pain during urination stopped and the fever disappeared. The antibiotics seemed to be working. The call from the doctor came that afternoon when Jackie got home from school. The urine sample came back positive—there were *E. coli* bacteria in Jackie's urine causing what the doctor called an "uncomplicated UTI."

Jackie was instructed to complete the series of antibiotics and call back if the symptoms did not go away in a few days. "And call us if this ever happens again," the nurse on the phone explained. "We can get you treatment right away." That's comforting, thought Jackie. And she went on with her day.

COMMON SYMPTOMS

People with a UTI may experience some, none, or all of the common symptoms listed below. The American Urological Association and the Kidney Foundation of Canada list these symptoms as possible signs of a UTI:

- **Pain when urinating.** A burning pain in the urethra or bladder is not uncommon for those with UTIs. In her book *The Patient's Encyclopedia of Urinary Tract Infections, Sexual Cystitis and Interstitial Cystitis*, Kilmartin describes the pain while urinating as "shivery cold," "scalding," and "like broken glass," depending on the severity and stage of the infection.

- **Frequent and urgent need to urinate.** This symptom goes two ways: an inability to control when you urinate or an inability to urinate even when you feel the need. Both can occur with a UTI. Incontinence, the inability to control urination, forces the infected person to stay near a bathroom, while the inability to urinate creates stomach or bladder pain.
- **Bloody urine.** Blood from the walls of the urethra or bladder may be present in the urine. This happens more commonly in cases of repeated infection, where scars develop in the urinary tract and are easily reopened. If you see blood in your urine, you will likely start to feel worse soon.
- **Cloudy, milky, or foul-smelling urine.** Cloudy, milky, or foul-smelling urine can be caused by too many white blood cells in the urine, a sign that the immune system is working overtime.

LESS COMMON SYMPTOMS

If a UTI is allowed to progress without treatment, or if an individual's response to the infection is strong, look for these less common symptoms, provided by the National Kidney and Urologic Disease Information Clearinghouse in the United States:

- **Back or side pain.** Both men and women may feel UTI-induced pain in the back or in the side just below the ribs from kidney infection. In addition, women can feel pain in the bladder or urethra even when not urinating. Some men experience a fullness of the rectum.

- **Fever.** A UTI-related fever may indicate that the infection has spread to the kidneys and should be diagnosed and treated immediately. Children with UTIs are likely to have a fever and no other symptoms.
- **Nausea.** Nausea combined with general fatigue, sluggishness, and loss of energy can be a sign of a

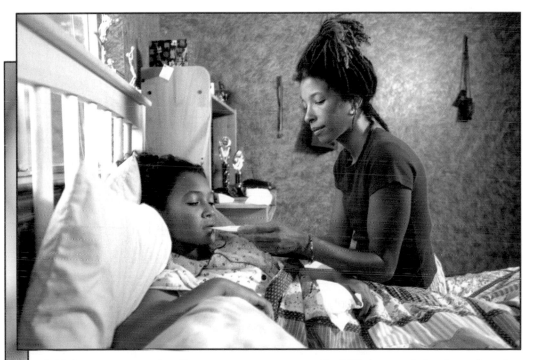

A high temperature is a less common symptom of a UTI, but an infection-related fever is not rare. For some people, especially for children, a fever is the only symptom that tells a doctor that the patient has a UTI.

UTI. Nausea can also be a sign that a UTI has spread to the kidneys.

LENGTH OF SYMPTOMS

Once you identify a symptom or symptoms of a UTI, how long do you wait before taking action? Expert advice varies and there is no reliable rule.

Most organizations suggest calling the doctor as soon as you suspect a UTI. Others suggest waiting twenty-four hours if you have any common symptoms of a UTI. If symptoms persist after this time, then make an appointment to see a doctor. In recurrent cases, a doctor may prescribe a treatment of antibiotics over the phone without even seeing the patient. According to Paul Iannini's book *Contemporary Diagnosis and Management of Urinary Tract Infections*, research shows that symptoms caused by uncomplicated UTIs last about six days, including two days of missed work or school. By this time, people either receive treatment and feel better or the infection and symptoms become worse.

Though expert opinions vary, it is hard to argue against taking immediate action if you suspect a UTI. Call your doctor to be safe.

CHAPTER FOUR

Getting Help for a UTI

People might not want to talk about UTIs, but millions of people get them every year: men and women, young and old. Chances are a UTI won't go away by itself—it will only get worse. If you suspect that you have a UTI, the following information explains what to expect and what to do.

DEALING WITH A UTI

You (and everyone who gets a UTI) will need help fighting this infection. You can't conquer it alone no matter how strong you are. It can be awkward and inconvenient, but there's no need to feel ashamed.

Step one is to find a parent, reliable friend, teacher, school counselor, or nurse whom you trust. Tell them your symptoms and that you suspect a UTI. They may or may not have useful UTI information, but you could find out that you are not alone. If nothing else, talking to someone helps you practice what you want to say for a visit to the doctor.

- Have you ever had a UTI?
- Are you allergic to any medications?
- Are you sexually active?

The answers to these questions can help the doctor diagnose the infection or know what else to look for.

Giving a Urine Sample

If the doctor suspects that you have a UTI, he or she will request a urine sample to see if bacteria are present in the urine. When you give a sample, you will be asked to give a "midstream" urine sample. The nurse will probably give you a sealed, sterile sample cup and instructions, or there will be instructions in the bathroom where you give your sample.

Basically, a midstream sample should give the doctor a "clean" sample, uninfected by bacteria on the skin outside the urethra. The procedure will read something like this:

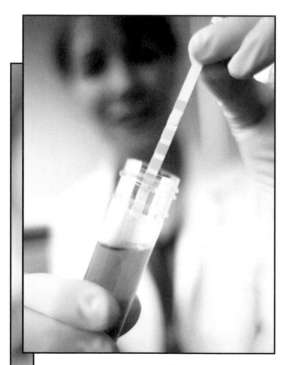

A technician uses a dipstick to test a urine sample for signs of a UTI.

First wash your hands. Next clean the skin around the opening of your urethra using cotton or sterile cloths provided by the nurse. Begin to urinate in the toilet, then stop (if possible) and place the cup in the stream. This flushes away any urine falsely contaminated with bacteria from your skin. Continue to urinate until you fill the sample cup as needed. Remove the cup from the stream. Then finish urinating, seal the cup, and wash your hands.

The urine will be tested to see if there are bacteria growing. Some doctors' offices are equipped to do a simple dipstick test. A dipstick test is a lot like a home pregnancy test; the end of a stick is dipped in urine and changes color instantly if bacteria are present. Some dipsticks detect nitrite, a substance produced by bacteria. Others detect the presence of white blood cells, another indication of a UTI.

Most offices will send the urine sample to a laboratory to be analyzed. If bacteria are present, they will be extracted from the urine and grown, producing larger bacteria populations called cultures. Different antibiotics are then tested on the cultures to see which drugs are best at killing that type of bacteria. This tells the doctor which antibiotic to prescribe to best fight the infection and saves you from taking drugs that won't work.

The dipstick test can be done immediately, while you wait. The laboratory test and culture might take a couple of days. Once the tests are completed, you can ask to see the results yourself. You can learn more about the particular kind of infection that is in your system, especially if it is a recurring one. If it is caused by bacteria that you have had before, perhaps you never got rid of your previous infection. If you aren't sure, this information could help you understand where the infection came from. You can talk about ways to prevent the infection with your doctor.

Getting Examined

In addition to asking questions and requesting a urine sample, some doctors may perform a physical exam. Whether or not this is done depends on the severity of your symptoms and on your doctor.

During the physical exam, the doctor will likely check your blood pressure and temperature, and take your height and weight measurements to gauge your overall health. The doctor may check for abdominal tenderness, pushing on different areas of your stomach to see if the kidneys or bladder are sensitive. A genital exam to check for tenderness and signs of infection may also be performed.

For some people, the genital exam is the most uncomfortable part of the visit. While nothing the doctor does should be painful—just looking and touching lightly—it can be awkward to be exposed and examined from the waist down. If this makes you uneasy, ask your doctor if the physical exam can wait until after the results of the urine test are known. If the test indicates an uncomplicated

UTI, the doctor may simply prescribe antibiotics and not need to perform a genital exam. What actually happens when you visit the doctor for a UTI depends largely on the individual and on the doctor.

If you want to know what your UTI visit will include, ask questions when you make an appointment. The person making the appointment may not have all the answers, but he or she can put you in contact with

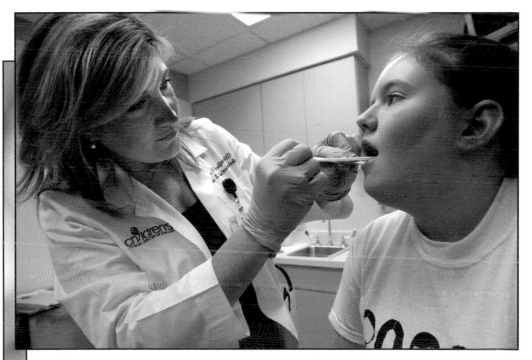

When you see the doctor for a UTI, expect a general physical exam that includes taking your blood pressure and temperature, and measuring your height and weight. These results are used to gauge your overall health.

nurses or others who can give you more information. Each doctor is different regarding how he or she structures the visit and physical examination.

DON'T IGNORE IT

It's easy to ignore a mild UTI. The inconvenient symptoms seem to go away on their own, only to surface again in a week or so, leading to a repeated cycle of infection. A persistent UTI is one that never goes away entirely. A recurrent UTI is one that is treated completely and then a new infection occurs. Such repeat infections can be caused by the same bacterial infection coming and going, or by new infections, each caused by a different type of bacteria.

According to *Contemporary Diagnosis and Management of Urinary Tract Infections*, young women who get a UTI have a 30 to 50 percent chance of getting another one. The chances are highest in the first month after the initial infection and then decrease the following year. There are no similar statistics currently available on young men.

Left untreated, repeat UTIs that spread to the kidneys can lead to a condition called chronic pyelonephritis, an infection of the kidneys that can lead to kidney failure. In a healthy urinary tract, the ureters rhythmically squeeze urine down from the kidneys. During urination the ends of the ureters are compressed where they enter the bladder, preventing urine from squirting up into the kidneys. Bacteria from infected urine in the bladder can travel up the ureters to infect the kidneys.

Repeated invasions of infected urine cause chronic pyelonephritis and possible kidney failure. When the kidneys fail, they cannot do their usual job of removing excess fluid and waste from your blood. Without these working filters, you build up dangerous levels of waste in your body. The scary thing about chronic pyelonephritis is that patients have few symptoms, not realizing they are approaching kidney failure until it's nearly too late.

According to information provided by the Mayo Clinic in Rochester, Minnesota, in 2004, many people don't realize they are close to kidney failure until the kidney functions are less than 25 percent normal. Furthermore, when kidney functions fall to 10 percent, the body simply cannot sustain life. At this point the patient needs dialysis (an artificial way of removing waste from the body) or a kidney transplant to stay alive.

CHAPTER FIVE

Living with a UTI

In most cases, the physical symptoms of UTIs can be effectively controlled with drug or nondrug treatments. The emotional symptoms and side effects of a UTI can be harder to control, as there aren't many support groups that recognize the condition. Here's a rundown of some physical and emotional treatment options.

DRUG TREATMENT

Antibiotics cured 85 percent of uncomplicated UTIs, according to the University of Maryland Medical Center in Baltimore, Maryland, in 2002. An antibiotic is a drug that kills bacteria or prevents them from multiplying. The type of antibiotic you take depends on the type of bacteria causing your infection; certain antibiotics kill certain types of bacteria. Taking the wrong antibiotic may not only be ineffective against the infection, it could actually make things worse.

The biggest concern about taking antibiotics for UTIs today is bacterial resistance. When you take an antibiotic, the drug kills the defenseless bacteria and leaves behind those able to resist it. The bacteria able to resist the antibiotic are slightly different from their defenseless siblings—a natural, evolutionary difference between organisms. Over time, only the bacteria able to resist the antibiotic survive and multiply, creating populations of infections that are immune to modern drugs. One example is the antibiotic amoxicillin, which used to be the standard UTI drug treatment prescribed by doctors. Today, as

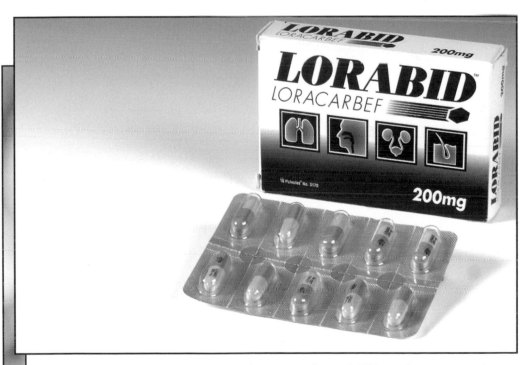

Antibiotics are a common treatment for uncomplicated UTIs and come in many varieties. Your doctor will choose the antibiotic that is right for you based on your type of infection. Lorabid (chemical name loracarbef), taken orally as a pill, is often used in killing the bacteria that cause UTIs in children.

reported by the University of Maryland Medical Center in 2002, amoxicillin is ineffective against *E. coli* in 25 percent of all UTI cases.

To slow bacterial resistance, doctors make every effort to give patients the correct antibiotic for the appropriate amount of time. The longer a patient takes the drugs, the longer the bacteria have to learn to evolve and resist treatment.

COMMON UTI DRUGS

In the past, ten days of antibiotic treatment for an uncomplicated UTI was typical. Today, that has been reduced to three days. The kind of antibiotic you take and how long you have to take it depends on your infection.

The following antibiotic suggestions are from the University of Maryland Medical Center, as reported in 2002. Specific recommendations and prescriptions vary depending on the individual patient's needs and on the doctor.

Antibiotic: TMP-SMX (trimethoprim-sulfamethoxazole)
Type of infection: Typical three-day treatment for uncomplicated UTIs
Concerns: Allergies to this drug can be serious (experts note that allergies to all drugs can be serious)

Antibiotic: Fluoroquinolones
Type of infection: Alternative treatment for uncomplicated UTIs

Concerns: Effective against a wide range of bacteria but is expensive; usually only used when TMP-SMX doesn't work

Antibiotic: Nitrofurantoin
Type of infection: Uncomplicated UTIs
Concerns: Treatment lasts more than three days; effective against many types of bacteria

Antibiotic: Tetracyclines
Type of infection: Uncomplicated or complicated UTIs
Concerns: Long-term course of antibiotic treatment with unusual side effects including sensitivity to sunlight, tooth discoloration, and possible burning in the throat

Antibiotic: Aminoglycosides
Type of infection: Complicated UTIs
Concerns: Given by injection for very serious infections

NONDRUG TREATMENT

There are no proven nondrug treatments that rid the body of bacterial infection, but there are many recommended practices that might be beneficial for some people. The nondrug treatments are harmless, but again, none of these practices should replace a visit to the doctor when UTI treatment is needed.

Many doctors believe that thoroughly cleansing the bladder daily can help rid the body of infection. They

One vaccine, called Urovac, is designed to fight UTIs in women and is already being tested in clinical trials. Urovac is a vaginal suppository composed of ten common UTI-causing bacteria. Initial test results are promising. According to a report in 2004 by the University of Maryland Medical Center, 55 percent of the women who received the vaccine plus a follow-up booster remained free of UTIs for six months, while only 22 percent of the women who got a placebo, or dummy, vaccine or the vaccine without follow-ups remained free of UTIs for the same six months. Urovac appears to help fight UTIs without side effects, but research is ongoing. Scientists are also working on a different type of vaccine that prevents *E. coli* from attaching to the walls of the bladder—a vaccine that would work in both men and women.

If you suffer from recurrent UTIs, ask your doctor about vaccine options. Currently, vaccines are not readily available to treat UTIs, but the field is changing rapidly.

EMOTIONAL TREATMENT

Although there is much attention paid to the physical treatment of UTIs, there are very few, if any, emotional support groups devoted to teen sufferers of urinary tract infections in the United States. Your best bet is to find someone you know and trust—a parent, friend, relative, or other loved one—with whom you can speak. Chances are your peers may have dealt with the same problems even if no one is talking about them.

You can find organizations and formal UTI support groups, but be prepared: finding a group may take a lot of research and time. Start at your doctor's office. Ask the nurse or doctor if there are any UTI support groups in your area. If the doctor or nurse is unable to recommend any, ask for the name of a urologist in the area that you can call. Ask the urologist the same question—if he or she doesn't know whether there is a group in your community, the urologist will probably know where to look for the nearest one.

A group of teens with assorted urological diseases meets to talk with a counselor. People who have UTIs need not suffer alone. Listening to others' experiences and sharing your own can help you learn more about UTIs and treatment options.

FOR FURTHER READING

Columbia University's Health Education Program. *The "Go Ask Alice" Book of Answers: A Guide to Good Physical, Sexual, and Emotional Health*. New York, NY: Henry Holt & Company, 1998.

Fullick, Ann. *Body Systems and Health*. Chicago, IL: Heinemann-Raintree, 2006.

Kilmartin, Angela. *The Patient's Encyclopedia of Urinary Tract Infection, Sexual Cystitis and Interstitial Cystitis*. Chula Vista, CA: Bay Port Press, 2004.

Krohmer, Randolph. *The Reproductive System* (Your Body: How It Works). New York, NY: Chelsea House Publishers, 2003.

Manning, Shannon. *Escherichia coli Infections*. New York, NY: Chelsea House Publishers, 2004.

Sarnoff Schiff, Harriet. *The Support Group Manual: A Session-by-Session Guide*. New York, NY: Penguin Books, 1996.

Simone, Catherine. *To Wake in Tears: Understanding Interstitial Cystitis*. Cleveland, OH: IC Hope Limited, 1998.

Stanley, Deborah A. *Sexual Health Information for Teens*. Detroit, MI: Omnigraphics, 2003.

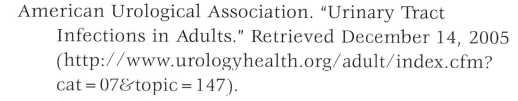

BIBLIOGRAPHY

American Urological Association. "Urinary Tract Infections in Adults." Retrieved December 14, 2005 (http://www.urologyhealth.org/adult/index.cfm? cat=07&topic=147).

Freedman, Andrew L. "Urinary Tract Infection in Children." In *Urologic Diseases in America*, Mark S. Litwin and Christopher S. Saigal, eds. U.S. Department of Health and Human Services, Public Health Service, National Institutes of Health, National Institute of Diabetes and Digestive and Kidney Diseases. Washington, DC: U.S. Government Printing Office, 2004.

Iannini, Paul. *Contemporary Diagnosis and Management of Urinary Tract Infections*. Newtown, PA: Handbooks in Healthcare Co., 2003.

Kidney Foundation of Canada. "Urinary Tract Infections." Retrieved November 5, 2005 (http://www.kidney.ca/ english/publications/brochures/urinarytract/ urinarytract.htm).

Kilmartin, Angela. *The Patient's Encyclopedia of Urinary Tract Infection, Sexual Cystitis and Interstitial Cystitis*. Chula Vista, CA: Bay Port Press, 2004.

Manages, Amee. Interview by Krista West, December 16, 2005.

Mayo Clinic. "Diabetes." May 13, 2004. Retrieved
    November 22, 2005 (http://www.mayoclinic.com/
    health/kidney-failure/DS00280).

MedLinePlus. "Urinary Tract Infections." August 4, 2005.
    Retrieved November 11, 2005 (http://www.nlm.nih.
    gov/medlineplus/ency/article/000521.htm).

National Kidney and Urological Diseases Information
    Clearinghouse. "Urinary Tract Infections in Adults."
    December 2005. Retrieved December 29, 2005 (http://
    kidney.niddk.nih.gov/kudiseases/pubs/utiadult/).

Penn State Children's Hospital. "Urinary Tract Infections."
    Retrieved December 29, 2005 (http://www.hmc.psu.
    edu/childrens/healthinfo/uz/uti.htm).

Roach, John. "Antibiotic Beer Gave Ancient Africans
    Health Buzz." National Geographic News. May 16,
    2005. Retrieved December 2, 2005 (http://news.
    nationalgeographic.com/news/2005/05/0516_
    050516_ancientbeer.html).

University of Maryland Medical Center. "How Are
    Antibiotics Used in Treating Urinary Tract Infections?"
    September 30, 2002. Retrieved December 27, 2005
    (http://www.umm.edu/patiented/articles/what_a_
    urinary_tract_infection_000036_8.htm).

University of Maryland Medical Center. "Urinary Tract
    Infections." September 30, 2002. Retrieved December
    27, 2005 (http://www.umm.edu/patiented/articles/
    what_a_urinary_tract_infection_000036_1.htm).

INDEX

A

age, and UTIs, 18–20
antibiotics, 5, 23, 29, 34, 39, 41, 44–47

B

bacteria
    antibiotics and, 44–46
    in digestive system, 9, 11, 14
    in reproductive system, 13–14, 22
birth control, 7, 11, 15, 18, 22–24

C

catheters, 20–21, 22, 24
cystitis, 15

D

diabetes, 21, 22

E

E. coli, 11, 13, 15, 22, 23, 46, 50

H

health, and UTIs, 21–22

K

kidneys, problems with, 5, 16, 21, 22, 32, 33, 34, 42–43

P

pregnancy, 21–22, 24
pyelonephritis, 16, 42–43

S

support groups, 29, 44, 50–52

U

urethritis, 15
urinary tract infections
    causes of, 4, 7, 9, 11–14, 15, 20, 22–24
    complicated, 4–5, 14, 15–16
    emotions and, 5, 35, 44, 50–51
    getting help for, 34, 35–43
    myths about, 10
    preventing, 10, 24–27
    statistics on, 4, 6, 17, 18, 23
    symptoms of, 4, 10, 15, 16, 29, 31–34
    treatment for, 5, 23, 34, 39, 44–50
    uncomplicated, 4, 14–15, 34
urinary tract system, about, 7–9
urine sample, giving a, 38–39

W

women, and UTIs, 6, 9–11, 17, 18, 21–24, 25, 42, 50

ABOUT THE AUTHOR

Krista West is among the 20 percent of women who develop a urinary tract infection at some point in their lifetime. Luckily, her infection was uncomplicated, not contagious, and easily treated with antibiotics. She combined her personal UTI experience with her work as a science writer for young adults to complete this book. Ms. West is a graduate of the Earth and Environmental Science Journalism program at Columbia University, specializing in health, ecology, and earth science.

PHOTO CREDITS

Cover, p. 4 © www.istockphoto.com/ericsphotography; cover, pp. 1, 4 (silhouette) © www.istockphoto.com/jamesbenet; p. 1 (inset) CDC; p. 5 © Bob Pardue/Alamy; p. 8 © Roger Harris/Photo Researchers, Inc.; p. 12 © Eye of Science/Photo Researchers, Inc.; p. 15 © John Bavosi/Photo Researchers, Inc.; p. 19 © age fotostock/SuperStock; p. 20 © Josh Sher/ Photo Researchers, Inc.; p. 26 © KRT/NewsCom; p. 28 © Ron Chapple/ PictureArts/NewsCom; p. 33 © Bob Daemmrich/The Image Works; p. 36 © Richard Lord/The Image Works; p. 38 © Ian Hooton/Science Photo Library/Photo Researchers, Inc.; p. 41 © AP/Wide World Photos; p. 45 © Patricia Miller/The Medical File/Peter Arnold, Inc.; p. 48 © www. istockphoto.com/Gloria-Leigh Logan; p. 51 © Mary Kate Denny/ PhotoEdit; back cover (top to bottom) CDC/Dr. E. Arum, Dr. N. Jacobs, CDC/Dr. Edwin P. Ewing, Jr., CDC/Joe Miller, CDC/Joe Miller, CDC/ Dr. Edwin P. Ewing Jr., CDC.

Designer: Nelson Sá; **Editor:** Kathy Kuhtz Campbell
Photo Researcher: Amy Feinberg